Mike,

Keep growing!

Chris Loflin

10/14/2019

Praise for Jones Loflin and *Always Growing*

"*Always Growing* serves as a poignant reminder that all relationships – business as well as personal – are living things. As such, following a proven regimen of care and nurturing is essential to their continued success. The book's practical and well-explained analogies are helpful for leaders in any circumstance. Additionally, the use of relatable characters and scenarios makes the book an absolutely enjoyable read. For both new and experienced leaders alike, this book is an eye-opener to the boundless possibilities of intentional leadership!"

> – Leslie C. Cooper, Esq.
> *Deputy Director/Chief Operating Officer*
> *Pretrial Services Agency for the District of Columbia*

"Anyone in a leadership role will benefit from *Always Growing*. It's an effortless read introducing concepts (and reinforcing existing ones) on how to powerfully manage a team."

> – Craig Mueller
> *Manager, Coach: Training & Development*
> *Tractor Supply Company*

"Jones Loflin has impressive and entertaining messages that all individuals in any line of business or walk of life MUST hear."

> – Kathi Newman
> *CMPE and President*
> *Medical Group Management Association of Utah*

Always Growing

How To Be
A Strong(er) Leader
In Any Season

Jones Loflin

ELUCIDATE
PUBLISHING

SALT LAKE CITY

LIBRARY OF CONGRESS CONTROL NUMBER: 2016916101

ISBN 978-0-9766882-3-5

10 9 8 7 6 5 4 3 2

Always Growing may be purchased in bulk for educational, business, fundraising or sales promotional use. For information, email the author at orders@jonesloflin.com or call 800-853-4676.

For more information on keynotes and training programs
related to *Always Growing*:
800-853-4676 • www.alwaysgrowingbook.com

To my dad,
who first instilled within me
a love for seeing things grow.

"We keep bringing in mechanics —
when what we need are gardeners.
We keep trying to drive change —
when what we need to do is cultivate change."

– PETER SENGE

Author of *The Fifth Discipline* and *The Dance of Change*

"Before you are a leader,
success is all about growing yourself.
When you become a leader,
success is all about growing others."

– JACK WELCH

Author and Former CEO of General Electric

Table of Contents

NEEDING TO GROW

"What was I thinking?" "Have I lost my mind?" "Have I doomed my career?" These and more frantic thoughts raced through David's mind as he sped down the interstate. He wanted to be excited but, after the initial meeting about his new job, he wondered if he really had made the right decision.

David had been the "go-to guy" for troubleshooting problems and finding solutions at Trendex. His hard work, technical skills and attention to detail led to success in previous positions. It seemed like he had the perfect situation – that was, until he grew tired of the frequent travel, long hours and inconsistent schedule.

David also sensed that he was ready for something more. In past roles, he typically worked alone, interacting with others only when necessary to solve a problem or get more information. In his work with Trendex and its customers, he encountered teams that really seemed to know how to get things done. David admired the men and women who led such teams and wondered if he could become that kind of leader.

His desire to take his career in a new direction led David to apply for a division manager position at the Trendex facility on the east coast, even though it would require relocating his family. He knew it was a long shot, but a recent reorganization had created several vacancies.

To his surprise, David got the job. While he wouldn't start the new position until next month, the company asked him to visit the facility today to get a better understanding of its operations and his team.

In talking with the vice president of his division, David discovered the group he was now responsible for had been plagued by poor leadership. The company had overlooked its poor performance in the past but, with the uncertain economy, there were no guarantees. David knew that if he didn't get his team moving in the right direction fast, he might be out of a job.

David's biggest realization to this point was that it was going to be incredibly difficult to get his work done AND figure out how to best help his team members get their work done too. David thought to himself, "If I'm feeling this way *before* I start, what's it going to be like when it's for real?"

David's reflection about this season of change in his life brought him back to thoughts of his family. The new job at Trendex required David to relocate and, while he was excited about the possibility of new beginnings, the uncertainty of it all was a bit overwhelming. He sighed and thought, "Ashley is already in middle school, and Emma is turning 5 next month." David knew that there were some things he just didn't want to miss as a dad. "I've got to make this new direction work out," he murmured to himself.

And then there was his amazing wife, Amy. Time with her was always too short. Her success as a teacher was well-known, but her long hours and their joint responsibilities as parents only further limited their ability to grow in their relationship as a couple. These days it seemed as if they spent a lot more time reflecting on how good things *used* to be, before life got so crazy. Unfortunately, the new job and the move were adding even more stress to their relationship.

David exited the interstate and turned left at the intersection. The two-lane road with minimal traffic gave him a moment to relax and enjoy the view of familiar rolling hills. Stopping for a moment to get out and stretch, he took in the chilly fresh air as he stood up and thought, "This trip back to where I grew up is just what I need to clear my head." After a few moments, he got back behind the wheel and chuckled, "Kelly is going to be so surprised."

Kelly and David grew up like typical siblings, even though they were nine years apart. They fought one minute and were inseparable the next. He laughed out loud thinking about some of the pranks and practical jokes they had pulled on each other.

He and Kelly remained close through his high school years but began to drift apart after their mom lost her battle with cancer and their dad took a job in another state. David's career had taken him to the west coast, leaving little opportunity to return to where he grew up. Despite good intentions, visits occurred only about once a year…but that was about to change.

David's new job was at the Trendex facility about an hour from Kelly and her husband Michael's home. David was looking forward to seeing Kelly more often because moments with her were never dull, and she always seemed to have time to engage in meaningful conversation. As he turned right at the "Kelly's Place" sign, rows of apple trees and open fields reminded him of one of her true passions.

EXPERIENCING A
GREEN THUMB EPIPHANY

From the time she was 4 years old, Kelly loved watching things grow. Their grandfather was an avid gardener and apple grower, and Kelly definitely inherited his genes. She was always finding seeds and sticking them in the dirt or, as she later reminded David, "Soil. It's called soil. Dirt is what you get on your pants."

She nurtured her green thumb throughout her teenage years, eventually establishing her own roadside vegetable stand. After high school, she continued to expand her operation while attending the local community college. Following graduation, she purchased some land with the help of their dad and combined it with acreage from their grandfather's farm to establish an apple orchard and commercial fruit and vegetable operation.

Kelly was now one of the largest produce growers in the region. She was extremely intelligent, understood horticultural practices better than people twice her age and had an incredible work ethic. What accelerated the growth of her business more than anything, however, was her uncanny ability to work with people. She just knew how to bring out the best in others.

David parked his car at the retail center. There wasn't a significant amount of produce for sale at this time of year, so there were only a few customers in the store.

As he wandered the aisles, his eyes were drawn to the "Growers of Tomorrow" wall, which showcased numerous pictures of children and adults showing off fruits and vegetables they had grown. As he moved closer, he began reading a letter to Kelly from someone who had started his own vegetable operation because of her guidance. He chuckled to himself, "That's one way to put yourself out of business."

His musing was interrupted by the sound of footsteps. One of Kelly's employees approached him and said, "Good afternoon. I'm Maria. How may I help you?"

David put on a serious face and asked, "Is the owner here?"

Maria answered, "Why yes, she is."

"Good," David said. "I want to speak to her. I bought some apples here a month ago, and they rotted within a week."

Maria seemed shocked but held her composure. "I'm so sorry, sir," she replied. "Let me page Kelly so you can share your concern with her."

David could hardly keep from breaking out in laughter as he thought about Kelly and her reaction when she found out who the angry customer was. He didn't have to wait very long.

Kelly came scurrying through the door, drying her hands with a towel as she approached the service counter to talk with Maria. David moved out of sight for just a moment so she couldn't see him.

As Kelly finished speaking to Maria, David stepped out from behind a tall display of seed packets, and Kelly's tanned face erupted into a huge smile. "YOU!" she exclaimed. "You never quit, do you?"

After a quick hug, Kelly motioned for Maria to join them. "Maria, this is my brother, David – the world's *worst* practical joker."

Maria extended her hand and smiled. "We've heard some stories about the two of you," she said.

"I'm sure they get better with time," David replied.

"Now if you'll excuse me, I need to go take care of our next *crisis*," Maria chuckled. "It was nice meeting you." David smiled in response as she returned to the counter.

Turning their attention to each other, Kelly said, "What a wonderful surprise, David! But what in the world are you doing here? I hope nothing's wrong."

"Oh no," David replied. "In fact, I have good news. Seems as if you'll be seeing more of me in the near future."

Kelly smirked and said, "I thought you said you had GOOD news." Smiling warmly, she then said, "I can't wait to hear about it. Give me about five minutes to give instructions to some of my team members, and then we can meet in the office."

David paused at the bulletin board hanging at the entrance to Kelly's office. Pictures of employees and their families covered much of the space. There were wedding announcements, baby pictures and other life-related invitations. Near the center of the board was a faded piece of paper that read, **"You are always a gardener. What grows – and how it grows – is up to you."** It was her favorite saying.

"Good-looking bunch, eh?" Kelly asked as she came through the door.

"Certainly is, sis," David replied. "You've done well."

You are always a gardener.
What grows—and how it grows—
is up to you.

"Thanks, David," she said. "Now tell me what brings you back to our little corner of the world."

They sat down at a small conference table, and David shared more about his new job as division manager and returning to the area.

"Well, that sounds like fantastic news," Kelly said. "I know Amy and the kids will be happy to see more of you and start a new chapter in their lives."

"Yes," David replied. "That's the upside. The downside is that for the first time in my career, much of my work is about leading and managing others. I'm not sure I'm cut out to tell other people what to do."

Kelly leaned forward and said, "If that's your idea of leadership, I can assure you that your time in that position will be short."

David tried to clarify his comment. "That came out wrong," he said. "What I mean is that I'm accustomed to lining up my own work and doing it without relying on much help from others. All of my focus has been on me. As a division manager, I'm going to be responsible for making sure my entire team is working on the right things. THAT stresses me out in a way I can't begin to explain."

"Well," Kelly began, "maybe a visit here every now and then can help with that new job. And who knows… you might just 'grow' a little while you're here."

"What do you mean?" David asked.

"I know it may sound strange, but I've found that many principles of growing successful plants can be applied to leading teams and managing people," Kelly explained.

David laughed out loud and then replied, "Kelly, I think you've been hanging out in the greenhouse a little too long."

"I'm serious," Kelly replied with a sharper tone. "Things like identifying what causes something to grow, knowing how to provide a positive environment and using your resources wisely are critical whether you're running a company or growing award-winning apples."

Sensing he might have touched a nerve, David conceded. "Well, I can't deny you've grown something here that's been successful for many years," he said. "And right now, I need all the help I can get. So if you're willing to offer advice, I'm willing to listen."

Kelly stood up. "Good. Let's take a quick walk," she said. "It will only take five minutes. Get your coat from the car, and meet me behind the greenhouses."

David was flooded with memories as he passed his grandfather's old hay barn on the way to the greenhouses. He and Kelly had spent many hours working, playing and daydreaming in there. As he turned to walk behind the greenhouses, Kelly joined him from the other direction.

"Where are we going?" David asked.

"You'll see."

They walked for another minute or so before arriving at a row of strange-looking old apple trees. Some were tall with only two or three towering branches, while others looked more like shrubbery with an untold number of limbs zigzagging their way around the trunk, making it almost impossible to identify a single branch. And in some spots, there were only stumps where trees had once stood.

"Not exactly your best work, I would hope," David said.

"No, but they are the *result* of my work," Kelly explained. "These were some of the first trees I planted on my own. I was going to show grandpa and everyone else that I knew what I was doing, but it was during high school, and I got busy and chose to spend my time on other things.

"I worked on them occasionally," she continued, "but eventually it was no use. I knew they couldn't produce the kind of apples I needed to sell. These trees had the potential to produce some fantastic apples, but I missed my chance because I was too busy with other things. I keep them here as a reminder of what NOT to do if you want to be a successful gardener. You have to **identify what you can and cannot control, and invest your time where you can have the greatest return.**"

Identify what you can and
cannot control, and invest your time
where you can have the
greatest return.

Pulling at a dead limb on one of the trees, Kelly continued. "Successful gardeners know that **letting something grow on its own doesn't always bring the desired result.** Just because you start something with good intentions doesn't mean it will turn out well. And, as you can see here, it often creates something you really *don't* want, especially if you make the wrong choices."

Letting something grow on its own doesn't always bring the desired result.

As they turned to walk back to the parking lot, David had to admit that Kelly's words stirred some thoughts about his own situation. Those trees, like the people he was leading, had the potential to create some great results if he chose to spend more time developing them instead of just trying to get his own work done. In fact, he was beginning to see that focusing on the growth of his team *is* his most important work.

"Hmmm," David said as they passed the old barn again. "I think I get what you mean. But I'm still not sure how growing plants can be as challenging as leading a team of people. They're two very different things."

"Really?" Kelly said knowingly. "Maybe you just have a lot to learn."

"Well, if there's anyone who knows about growing things, it's you, Kelly," David said. "I've got to run. Give my best to Michael."

"Yes, he will be so disappointed that he missed you. Give Amy and the kids a big hug for me."

"Will do," David replied as he hugged Kelly goodbye.

GROWING TIPS

- You are always a gardener. What grows – and how it grows – is up to you.

- Identify what you can and cannot control, and invest your time where you can have the greatest return.

- Letting something grow on its own doesn't always bring the desired result.

BREAKING GROUND

A few weeks had passed since David's introductory meeting with his new team at Trendex. He and the family had begun settling into their new community. There were still plenty of boxes to unpack, and Amy was busily searching for a new job.

At work, David found himself frequently comparing growing plants to leading people. And while he was spending time learning and applying more complex models to improve his leadership skills, Kelly's notion kept resurfacing with the most clarity of action.

"Okay, Kelly," he thought to himself. "You've bailed me out in the past; let's see if you can do it again." He took out an index card and wrote, "You are always a gardener. What grows – and how it grows – is up to you." He taped it to the edge of his computer monitor.

David made it a priority over the next few days to really listen to what his team members were saying in meetings as well as in individual conversations. As they talked with him, he heard Kelly's words again and again: *Letting something grow on its own doesn't always bring the desired result.*

"These people feel like no one really cared about how the work got done," he reflected. "It's no wonder they're struggling."

David scribbled a few notes to himself before his weekly team meeting. "Let's start being a little more intentional," he thought as he headed to the conference room.

He arrived 10 minutes early to find Keith already there.

"Hello, Keith," he said, taking the adjacent seat. "How's your Monday going?"

"Can't complain for 9:20," Keith replied. "But who knows what else the day holds?"

A few moments later, Felicia, Raj, Chris, Liam and Jerome filed in and took their seats. David moved to the front of the room and said, "I know our first few meetings have been more about getting to know each other and the work in front of us, but today I want to do something different."

He approached the whiteboard and wrote, "What will you grow today?" His team looked confused. He then verbalized the question.

He spent the next few minutes describing his "grower's mindset" about leadership and how he saw his primary role as being responsible for helping them grow. He concluded with, "And just as I see myself as being responsible for growing the right things, I see all of you as growers too. So what are *you* looking to grow today?"

An awkward silence fell over the room, but David didn't speak. He knew this step was critical to helping his team start being more purposeful about their work.

Finally, Felicia spoke up. "I've got an idea for improving one of our products," she said. Other members of the team slowly responded with various projects they were working on and ideas they had about potential tasks to accomplish.

"Good," David replied. "As you know, the stakes are higher for all of us. We're being watched more closely than ever to see if we can produce better results. And the only way we can make that happen is if we're more intentional about how we spend our time."

David took a few minutes to review the goals for their division. He then asked each team member to reflect on how the ideas they shared aligned with the goals. From there, he had each team member write a goal-oriented idea on the whiteboard and identify where he or she could have the greatest influence in making that idea a reality.

"In the coming days, I want you to do two things as you plan your work," David said as he began to debrief the exercise. "One is to be more conscious about reflecting on our goals. The second is to focus more of your time on the areas where you have greater control – or at least influence – in taking action to make these goals a reality.

"If we're thinking like growers, I guess I would say, if we're supposed to be growing tomatoes, let's make sure we're spending as much time as possible growing tomatoes," he concluded.

The discussion was moving along well until Jerome spoke up.

"What does this exercise have to do with getting better results?" he asked. "I still have to do all the other parts of my job. This extra step just seems to give me more work to do. That's exactly what I *don't* need!"

Before David could respond, Keith answered Jerome's question.

"The difference is that, using this mindset, I'll prioritize the things that will help me best 'grow' the results I'm expected to create as a team member and that we're expected to achieve as a team," Keith explained.

"Exactly," David responded. "It's about being more *intentional* in working on the things that will give you the best results. It's about choosing to work on them first and not last." Jerome nodded slowly in agreement.

After wrapping up a few administrative details, David ended the meeting. Chris stayed behind as everyone else walked out of the room. He closed the door and turned toward David.

"Nice talk," Chris said. "I guess that's the 'flavor of the month.' What will it be next? Comparing leadership to driving a car or maybe building a house?"

Picking up on Chris's negative attitude, David responded, "Actually, I plan to use this same approach for as long as it works…"

"And as long as you're here, right?" Chris interrupted.

"Well, yes," David replied.

Wanting to get off on the right foot with Chris, he sat down and said, "Chris, I sense some deeper frustration behind your words. Help me understand where that's coming from."

Chris sat down and took a deep breath. "I've been managing a team here for over 10 years. I've seen all kinds of models and analogies come and go, and I've had more bosses than I care to count. My philosophy is that you just do your job and hope for the best."

David thought for a moment and then said, "Chris, I respect your candor. I'm going to need that if we're going to get moving in the right direction. I want to learn from you. All I ask is that you give me some time to put this plan into action, and then let's see where it takes us."

Chris looked doubtful. "Okay. I'll give it a shot. But to use your analogy, don't be surprised when your ideas die for lack of water."

"Thanks, Chris," David responded with a smile. "That's all I ask."

Chris shrugged, stood up and walked out of the room.

David felt a little overwhelmed as he thought about what just happened. Even with Chris's resistance, he knew he had given his team the hope that they could achieve more than they had in the past. Now he just had to figure out exactly *how* to give them what they needed to make it happen. He trusted that an upcoming visit with Kelly would give him some answers.

REQUIRING MORE
THAN JUST SUNLIGHT

Arriving at Kelly's place in the afternoon, David found things to be a little different than on his last visit. People were planting seeds in the greenhouse, and he could see other employees in several of the surrounding fields.

Walking toward Kelly, who was working in a plant bed close to the parking lot, David said, "Wow! Things must be pretty tough around here. They've got the CEO getting her hands dirty."

Kelly pulled off one of her gloves and threw it playfully at David. "Maybe the problem is that you don't get that anything worth growing requires a lot of work," she said.

"Oh believe me, I'm beginning to see that," David replied. "Being a gardener or a leader isn't as easy as it looks."

She gave him a wink and said, "You catch on quicker than I thought. Let's go."

They walked to one of the storage buildings behind the office. Kelly handed David a pair of gloves as they began unloading some bags from a truck.

"Is all this fertilizer?" David asked.

"No. These bags are soil for the greenhouse plants," Kelly replied.

David grabbed one of the bags and easily tossed it in the cart.

"Wow!" he said. "That's really light. I expected a bag of dirt to be much heavier than that." Kelly gave him the evil look, and he sheepishly said, "I meant soil. Why is it so light?"

"It's specially mixed for the small trays used in a greenhouse," Kelly replied. "Every plant needs a specific environment to grow at its best. And that begins with the right soil. One that drains too quickly won't hold enough water for the plants to grow well. A soil that has too many clay particles will limit the oxygen available to the roots. You have to **create the environment that gives a plant the best chance to grow**."

Create the environment that gives a plant the best chance to grow.

After dropping the soil off at the greenhouses, they returned to the truck. Looking at all of the different bags of fertilizer, David asked, "Why so many different ones? Wouldn't just one type of fertilizer work for most plants?"

"I'll explain as we take these bags for the apple trees to the upper orchards," Kelly replied. "Hop in."

David went to the other side of the truck, slid in and closed the door as they started up the gravel road.

"Once you create the best soil environment possible for a plant, you have to **determine what a plant needs for *optimum* growth**," Kelly began. "As long as these apple trees get the minimum requirements, they'll show some level of growth. They just won't grow at the desired rate or produce the quality or amount of fruit we need to make them profitable."

"So… the fertilizer provides what's missing?" asked David.

Determine what a plant needs for *optimum* growth.

"To a degree," Kelly answered. "As long as the limiting factor is nutrient-related. If the limiting factor is water or sunlight, the answer probably wouldn't be fertilizer."

Kelly stopped the truck, and they began unloading the bags onto a trailer.

After they finished, Kelly rested on the side of the truck and continued the conversation from a few minutes earlier.

"Once the basic factors of soil, light and water are taken care of, we have to determine what combination of nutrients is best for the plant."

Kelly pointed to the bags of fertilizer on the pallet.

"See the numbers 25-10-5 on the bags? Those numbers indicate the amount of three key nutrients – nitrogen, phosphorus and potassium – in each bag," Kelly continued. "Some plants require a different amount of one nutrient or another to grow best. While these are the big three, there are a number of other nutrients that plants need to absorb through the soil if they are to produce the desired result. The key is to remember that **a plant will only grow as fast as its most limiting factor**."

Kelly's comment struck a chord with David. "So I can provide an overabundance of one nutrient, but if it's lacking a critical amount of another one, I still won't get the desired result?"

"You got it," Kelly replied. "You're not giving the plant what it most needs for the growth you desire."

As they drove back to the office, David looked out across the rolling hills. Kelly's explanation helped him recognize where some changes were needed in leading his team.

Up to this point, he hadn't really thought about his role in creating the right environment. He now recognized that frequently reminding his team of the consequences if they didn't improve was probably creating negative pressure. And Trendex's culture of frequently moving leaders from one place to another was not motivating his team to build trust with him.

─────────────────────────────

A plant will only grow as fast as its most limiting factor.

─────────────────────────────

The idea of plants needing differing amounts of nutrients to grow made sense to him as well. Jerome's needs as the newest member of his team were very different from those of Keith, who had been with Trendex for more than 25 years. "I can't just take a 'one size fits all' approach to working with them," he thought to himself. David knew he needed to identify what would help each team member bring his or her best efforts to work.

Kelly noticed David's deep reflection and swerved to hit a bump in the gravel road to shake him out of it. "Speak up," Kelly said, as David gave her a puzzled look. "What's on your mind?"

Jolted, David glared at her for a moment, then shifted in his seat as he asked, "What if you create the right environment AND provide the nutrients they need, but they *still* won't grow?"

Pulling up to the office, Kelly opened the truck door and said, "Come with me."

They walked into a greenhouse where employees were placing small seedlings into trays of soil. The warmth in the greenhouse had David removing his coat as they stopped at a table filled with trays of small tomato plants.

"Okay, David, here's a test for you," Kelly said. "Do these seedlings have everything they need to grow?"

"Let's see," David replied. "The soil looks good, they're getting plenty of sunlight, and they look well-watered. I'm not sure about the fertilizer."

"We actually add fertilizer to the water, so yes, they are getting the nutrients they need," Kelly responded.

"I'd say they have everything they need to grow well then," David said with confidence.

"Alright," Kelly said. "If that's the case, why don't we just grow them outside instead of in this greenhouse?"

David paused for a moment and then answered, "Because it's too cold."

"Yes!" Kelly replied. "**A plant needs the right temperature to encourage it to grow**. You can provide as much of the other resources as you want, but if there's no sense of urgency created by higher temperatures, seeds won't sprout and plants won't grow. And just as nutrient requirements vary, so does the temperature needed by different plants."

A plant needs the right temperature to encourage it to grow.

"So if I understand how that applies to leading my team," David said, "then I need to find what gives each team member a sense of urgency to take a desired action."

"Exactly," Kelly replied. "I used to believe that everyone was motivated by the same things as me. I soon realized I couldn't truly help them grow in their role here until I understood the perspective of each member of my team and their unique needs."

"Interesting," David replied. "And with that moment of horticultural wisdom, I need to be on my way home."

"Oh, don't leave, David. We haven't even begun to talk about macro and micro nutrients, photosynthesis or transpiration. I thought you wanted to know *everything*," Kelly said with a grin.

"I've had enough for one day," David said, touching his hands to his head. "My brain hurts from all of this learning. I come here to *reduce* my stress… not *increase* it."

After a quick hug, David walked to his car and headed to the highway.

MORE GROWING TIPS

- Create the environment that gives a plant the best chance to grow.

- Determine what a plant needs for *optimum* growth.

- A plant will only grow as fast as its most limiting factor.

- A plant needs the right temperature (motivation) to encourage it to grow.

ENCOURAGING GROWTH

The drive home gave David an opportunity to digest his time with Kelly. He was sure he would flunk a test about plant growth and nutrition, but he was beginning to more clearly see the parallels to improving his ability to be a strong leader. He reflected on what he had written on his tablet earlier that day:

- Leaders create the environment that gives their people the best chance to grow.

- As a leader, I need to determine what each team member needs to grow.

- I have to remember that each team member will only grow as fast as his or her most limiting factor.

- People need the right motivation to encourage them to grow.

David thought about the connections to his own situation. He began to understand that he also needed to create a different work environment for himself. In the past, he had been focused solely on checking tasks off his list each day. Moving forward, David was determined to be more relationship-minded. That included little things such as taking the time to check in on his team members more often and having more authentic conversations about them as people, not just as employees.

David chuckled as he looked at his last entry about "the right motivation." He saw now that his journey to becoming a division manager was a perfect example of that concept. Had he been content to stay in a technical role, he would not have considered taking a leadership position, but the right motivation caused him to seek a change.

As David looked out the window, his mind turned to Amy. All of this talk about growing brought to mind a conversation they had a few months ago. She mentioned her desire to start graduate work, and he had resisted the idea because of their crazy schedules and his possible job change.

"I can't just limit my focus as a leader to my work team," he thought. "Amy needs opportunities to grow as well." He made a mental note to talk with Amy about changes they could make to help her reach her goals.

Pulling into the driveway, David beamed as he glimpsed his three favorite girls waving enthusiastically at his arrival.

Felicia was the first one David met with upon returning to work the next day. He knew she was struggling more than other members of his team. Walking into her office, he asked how things were going.

"Okay, I guess," Felicia answered. "After our meeting a few weeks ago, I was excited. I focused on what I needed to make a priority, but now things have stalled. I keep trying to do things differently, but I'm falling back into the same routine."

"Don't be so hard on yourself," David replied. "I'm partly to blame. I should have given you more guidance and support when I asked you to be more intentional about working on your priorities. The good news is that you survived, and it's time to get things growing."

"I think you mean 'going,' don't you?" Felicia asked as she chuckled.

"No, actually I do mean *growing*," he replied. "Let me ask you a question. What would be the ideal environment for you to really get things moving forward for your area?"

Felicia sat back in her chair for a moment and said, "Hmm… a few less meetings would help. That would give me more time to focus on getting actual work done – and doing it well."

"Good start," David responded. "What else?"

Felicia hesitated for a moment and then said, "The security of knowing that it's okay to say no every once in a while. Every time I think I'm getting a handle on things and making strides toward improving things in my area, I get asked to take on something more. I really need to complete my current projects before I get involved in anything else. Sometimes I feel like I'm juggling elephants."

David hadn't expected this second response from Felicia. He thought she wanted the additional opportunities and never realized that they were actually hindering her from accomplishing her core objectives well. He made a few notes and then asked a second question: "What would you say is the most limiting factor to making this work?"

Felicia looked away for a moment and then replied, "That's a tough one. The easy answer would be time, but I think the better answer is for the leaders at Trendex to be more accepting of the fact that when you're growing something new, you have to move more slowly."

"Interesting," David said, making a few more notes. "And other than time, what are some resources you believe would help you deliver your best work?"

"Now *that* one is easy," Felicia replied. "If I had more opportunities to collaborate with my counterparts in other divisions, I know I could learn some things that would help me be more successful."

"Okay," David nodded in approval before continuing. "One final question: What would you say motivates you more than anything else about your work?"

Felicia glanced out the window for a moment and then turned to David and said, "I think it would be having a sense of accomplishment. I love it when I'm responsible for taking an idea and seeing it through to a successful outcome."

After making a few more notes, David wrapped things up.

"Felicia, I appreciate your honesty," he began. "It's one of the things I have come to admire about you and other members of the team.

"Regarding fewer meetings, I'll check with the rest of the team to see if we can shorten our weekly meetings and also try to improve our communication by email. If we can establish a guideline for weekly updates from everyone, we can avoid having to meet and listen to everyone's reports at one time. As for not adding to your workload, I'll try to do a better job of spreading the assignments to others in the office.

"Trendex's acceptance of slower progress is a little more difficult. There's not a lot I can do about that, mainly because the vice president over this division is so sensitive about any changes in results. What I *can* do is talk with him and let him know that he might see slow growth for a while, but assure him that a quicker pace is coming. I'll also see if there's an easy way to get you more engaged with your counterparts in other divisions, even if it's some type of regularly scheduled videoconference or conference call. Would that help?"

"Absolutely," Felicia replied. "That would relieve some of the pressure I've been feeling lately and maybe give me some new ideas. Who knows... I might even be able to 'grow' better results."

David chuckled. "You *have* been listening, haven't you? I wasn't sure if my 'leader as gardener' talk helped or not."

"Oh, it's been good for me," Felicia replied. "I often find myself asking, 'What did I grow today that's moving me toward my goals?' If I struggle to answer that question, I look at what I might need to do differently tomorrow or the next week."

David rose as he gathered his materials.

"Thanks for the encouragement, Felicia," he replied. She nodded in approval as David headed out the door.

David smiled to himself as he returned to his office. "That's one more grower for the cause," he thought as he sat down at his desk, made a few more notes about the meeting and turned to his next task. Little did he know that a new leadership challenge was just around the corner.

GETTING INTO THE WEEDS

After his talk with Felicia, David spent more time thinking about his own growth. He needed to take an honest look at his environment to see where improvements could help him be more effective.

One thought that quickly came to mind was his constant battle with procrastination. He was often excited about what the end result of an idea could bring but hesitated when he thought about implementation – and sometimes lost his motivation to think or act differently.

David decided that in order to keep himself accountable, he would tell more people in his "inner circle" about what he wanted to do. He also would set obtainable milestones for himself and always finish what he started, even if the results weren't exactly what he had envisioned. "Sometimes done is better than perfect," he reasoned.

As the weeks passed, David began to see positive results. Felicia implemented a number of changes. A meeting with Raj identified some opportunities for improvement. Jerome and Liam were experiencing better progress as a result of David asking them the same four questions he posed to the other team members:

- What's the environment that will help you deliver your best work?

- What else do you need to deliver your best work?

- What do you see as the most limiting factor to delivering your best work?

- What motivates you to deliver your best work?

As for Chris, David was making painfully slow progress. His "four question" meeting revealed little opportunity for change, mainly because Chris was so set on doing things the way he had done them in the past. However, David did learn that Chris was strongly motivated by recognition; he liked for others – especially those in higher levels of the organization – to acknowledge what he was doing right.

David also found some success on a personal level: He and Amy were again talking about Amy working on her master's degree. They recognized that what they needed most was someone to take care of Ashley and Emma when Amy needed to take a class online or work on assignments. They found someone in their neighborhood who, if David had other obligations, would be willing to look after the girls one or two nights a week. Amy was already looking at potential graduate programs.

For a brief moment, David thought he was becoming a "master gardener" of life, but he soon found out there was much more to be learned.

It started with Keith, who stopped by David's office one day and shared that he was planning to retire in the next few months. Keith worked hard to keep things running smoothly but told David it was time to think about slowing down.

David kicked himself for not recognizing the potential for this to happen; Keith had even mentioned he was thinking of retiring some time ago. He really needed Keith's wisdom and insight right now.

Chris was the next one to need extra attention from David. He was having trouble keeping a consistent team of qualified technicians, and customer complaints about wait times and poor service were increasing. Thus far, Chris wasn't really open to suggestions from anyone.

But those challenges were small compared to the news he received from his vice president: Trendex was merging with another company, and the executive team overseeing the merger was considering cutting David's division because of a similar division in the other company.

Glancing at his calendar, David saw that he was scheduled to visit Kelly next week. With things being so crazy, he really wanted to cancel his visit, but something told him her world might reveal an idea or two to help with his new challenges.

TAKING CONTROL

Driving toward Kelly's house, David continued to struggle with feeling overwhelmed. "Having a growing mindset is all about giving people what they need," he mused. "And I'm doing that. Why aren't we moving forward more quickly?"

David pulled into Kelly's driveway and got his bag out of the car. Amy and the girls were away visiting her parents, so he decided to spend the night with Kelly and her husband, Michael, so they could get an earlier start the next morning. Michael met him at the door.

"Hey, it's the new hired hand!" Michael exclaimed. "Hope you're ready for some hard labor tomorrow."

"Work?" David retorted. "I come out here to *get away* from work."

"That's not what Kelly said. You'll have to take that up with her." He took David's bag to the guest bedroom, and Kelly emerged from the kitchen to hug David.

"Ready to go at it tomorrow?" she asked.

"I guess. More fertilizer to move?"

"Not exactly," she said. "I don't want you to think that everything we do around here is about having a strong back. Gardeners know that great results happen because of both physical AND mental hard work. Tomorrow is about cultivation."

"Cultivation?" David asked. "When I think of cultivation, I think of that piece of equipment grandpa pulled behind the tractor or the tiller we used in the garden at the house."

"You mean the tiller *I* used," Kelly replied. "I seem to recall *you* were always too busy with sports or something else to help out."

"Yeah, yeah, whatever," David said sarcastically. "Seriously, tell me more."

"We have plenty of time to talk shop tomorrow. How about some dessert before we call it a night?" Kelly asked.

"Depends on what you have," David said with a grin.

Michael yelled from the kitchen: "You know she only makes one dessert for you – apple crumble."

"In that case," David replied. "I'm in."

The next morning at breakfast, David was anxious to hear more about cultivation. Picking up his smartphone, he said, "One of the definitions I found was, 'To improve by labor, study or care.' How does that relate to growing plants or, more importantly for me, leading my team?"

Putting her fork down, Kelly began: "In my world, **cultivation is required to stay focused on what you want to grow.** I can't have my team just sow some seeds or put plants in the ground and then forget them. We have to monitor their growth, watch for problems and make adjustments as needed."

Cultivation is required to stay focused on what you want to grow.

She pointed to David's phone and continued: "To me, that definition of cultivation is perfect for anyone in a leadership role or working to grow something. To improve anything, you have to use your physical, mental and emotional resources."

Kelly stood up, moved her plate to the sink and said, "I think you'll understand better as we go through the morning. Let's get started."

David put his dishes in the sink, and they headed out the door.

The sun was shining brightly, and spring was in the air as they drove to a field covered in black plastic with ridges of green plants running the length of the field. The truck came to a stop as Kelly said, "See that plastic on the ground around the strawberry plants?"

"Sure," David replied.

"While the plastic helps with moisture retention for the roots, it also keeps weeds from growing around the plants because it takes away their ability to get light. We anticipate that weeds might be a problem and take action BEFORE they limit the growth of the strawberries," Kelly explained.

"Whatever the situation, it's important to remember that ***preventing* the weeds from growing limits their ability to use resources.** That strategy applies to insects, fungus and plant diseases as well. Identifying the problem early and addressing it quickly is key to keeping your plants healthy.

Preventing the weeds from growing limits their ability to use resources.

"You asked earlier about how the idea of cultivation applies to leadership," Kelly continued. "Over the years, I've come to realize that many problems a team experiences would never have been so draining to the team's performance if they had been addressed earlier."

After getting out to check on the strawberries, they returned to the truck and headed toward a field littered with dead leaves and stems from something that had previously grown there.

"Let's see how things are growing here," Kelly said as she hopped out of the truck and headed toward the field.

David strained to see any signs of green leaves. "How could anything grow with all this stuff on top of the ground?"

"That's just what I want to find out," Kelly said as she squatted closer to the ground. "There they are," she said with reassurance as she pointed to small sprouts of corn emerging from the ground. "Looks like we're okay so far."

"What do you mean?" David asked.

Standing up, Kelly said, "We tried something new this year when preparing the field to plant sweet corn. Normally, we would plow the ground or at least break up the soil with a tractor. It's just the way we had always done it.

"However, I noticed that farmers in the area have been using what's called 'no-till' on their large cornfields for years. When you plant that way, you don't plow the field. You use a mechanical planter that breaks up just enough of the soil to place the seed in the ground."

"What's the advantage of doing it that way?" David asked.

"Several things," Kelly responded. "One is that you leave more of this plant residue on the surface to hold moisture in the soil. Another is that you save money because you aren't using the tractor and plow to break up the soil and then going over it again to plant the seeds."

"Why hadn't you tried doing it that way in the past?" David asked.

"I just thought it was overkill for a small amount of land. But if it saves us a few dollars and reduces the amount of soil we lose to erosion, it's worth it. I'm still learning that it's a good idea to **continually evaluate your methods to see if they're making the best use of your resources.** Even a small change can have a big impact if multiplied by time or the number of people using it."

Continually evaluate your methods to see if they're making the best use of your resources.

David took a deep breath. Kelly's words reminded him of his ongoing challenge with Chris. He was adamant about doing things the way they had been done in the past, and it was hurting his team's performance.

David and Kelly spent the rest of the morning inspecting various fields of fruit and vegetable plants for pests and other problems. Each time they got back in the truck, Kelly would make notes on a tablet.

"You sure take a lot of notes," David said. "Is there really all that much you need to remember?"

Kelly glanced up from her notes and gave him a menacing look. "You didn't hear a word I said a few minutes ago, did you?"

David smiled and said, "Sure. You said that it was important to evaluate your methods."

"And just how am I supposed to evaluate my methods if I'm not keeping notes on my progress so I can compare it to previous years?" Kelly replied as she waved her pen in the air.

"Oh, I see," David said sheepishly. "It's like the quote from that management guru Peter Drucker: 'What gets measured gets managed.'"

"Yes," Kelly replied. "I know it seems like a lot right now, but when we want to compare our progress to previous years, this information becomes invaluable. It helps me see if the methods I'm using are working – or if we need to change."

Kelly looked at her watch. "We better get moving," she said as she started the truck. "My lunch date should be here any time."

As they approached the parking lot, David saw a twentysomething guy standing near the front door of the retail center.

"Hey, Aaron," Kelly said, rolling down her window. "Give us a second to wash up, and we'll be ready to go."

"Who's that?" David asked as they walked into the office.

"That's Aaron. He runs a large vegetable farm about an hour from here. I've been wanting to meet with him for weeks."

"Does Michael know about this?" David asked humorously.

"Very funny," Kelly replied.

On the way to the restaurant, David quickly learned that when you get two people together who have a love of growing plants, there's never a lull in the conversation. He could hardly get a word in as Kelly and Aaron exchanged ideas and pontificated about everything from controlling powdery mildew to their customers' newest vegetable craze.

"Wow! That was intense," David said when they returned from lunch. "I don't know who was more engaged, you or him."

"It's one of my favorite things to do," Kelly replied. "I've found that **time spent seeking advice and sharing ideas always helps you improve what you're growing**."

"I understand more now about this concept of cultivation," David said as he opened his car door. "We didn't exert a lot of physical energy today, but my brain has had a real workout."

"That's true," Kelly replied. "I've found that if I get too focused on *what* I'm trying to grow, I miss opportunities to improve *how* I'm growing it. And like that definition you found reminds me, improvement can only come when I'm willing to work, think and even care differently."

David sat down in his car and with a deep voice said, "I look forward to our next session of 'Growing with Kelly.'"

She rolled her eyes as he drove away.

Time spent seeking advice and sharing ideas always helps you improve what you're growing.

CULTIVATING TIPS

- Cultivation is required to stay focused on what you want to grow.

- *Preventing* the weeds from growing limits their ability to use resources.

- Continually evaluate your methods to see if they're making the best use of your resources.

- Time spent seeking advice and sharing ideas always helps you improve what you're growing.

WORKING THE TOUGH ROW

Over the next few days, David reflected on the concept of cultivation. "Keeping the focus on what you want to grow," he thought to himself. He even made a list of some "weeds" he saw trying to grow in his own world. They included:

- Increased mistakes created by the faster pace of his team
- Lack of time to think strategically
- Distractions related to the Trendex merger

As he reviewed the list, David remembered Kelly's tip about identifying what you can and cannot control. He knew that the pending merger was something over which he had no control, and he would just have to keep his team focused on its own goals. As for increased mistakes, David thought about creating some brief checklists that his team could use to help minimize missteps but still keep moving at a fast pace.

David was feeling somewhat overwhelmed. Trying to come up with specific strategies to stop or prevent these "weeds" from limiting the growth of his team seemed impossible. "This is one area where Kelly has it easy," he thought to himself. "All she has to do is identify the weed and either kill it or prevent new weed seeds from sprouting again."

Looking up from his notes, David paused for a moment. "Maybe that's it," he thought to himself. "If I could identify the 'seeds' of the weeds I'm facing, I could prevent them from growing in the future."

He stood up and moved to the whiteboard, where he wrote one "weed" on each of several sticky notes and attempted to group them. When he finished, there were three major areas.

"That helps a little," David thought, "but it still isn't what I need."

He reflected on some of the weeds in the first group.

"What do things such as 'disagreements with upper management' and 'unclear expectations' have in common?" he asked himself. "Priorities!" he said. "This first group of weeds shows up because of unclear priorities."

He wrote "Confused Priorities" at the top of the first group.

Moving on to the second group, he saw phrases such as "excessive workloads," "poor customer service" and "lack of collaboration."

"What's the common theme here?" he mused. "Every one of them is a... process!"

That was it! Each item in the group related to a process, system or procedure used by either Trendex or his team. David quickly wrote "Ineffective Processes" at the top of this group.

The last group had phrases that included "lack of motivation of one team member," "possible retirements" and "lack of trust." David quickly saw that this group was all about people. He wrote "People Challenges" at the top of the final group.

Stepping back to review his work, David felt a greater sense of clarity. He realized that the best way to help his team (and himself) stay focused on what they wanted to grow was to reflect on three key areas. He added a few questions he could ask himself while he was doing some cultivating at work:

Priorities

- Are our team priorities in alignment with the priorities of the organization?
- Does my team understand what our priorities are?
- Is my team fully focused on our priorities?

Processes

- Do our processes, systems and procedures support the goals we are trying to achieve?
- How does our way of doing something make it difficult for people to achieve their goals?
- What should we be doing differently to help people achieve their goals?

People

- Is the culture we have as a team creating the environment for people to deliver their best work?
- Am I meeting the needs of each team member?
- What do I see limiting the growth of any of my team members?
- Do I know the unique motivators for each person on my team?

This exercise was helpful for him personally, but it didn't yield any significant solutions for improving his team's performance.

Then, in reviewing his notes from the last visit with Kelly, he found his answer: "Time spent sharing ideas always helps you improve what you're growing."

David had told each of his team members that he saw them as gardeners, but now he wasn't asking for their input. "They know what they're trying to grow for their area better than I do. I should be asking them for *their* ideas," he thought to himself.

David started making notes for the next team meeting.

Walking into the meeting room, the team was surprised to find several pages of flipchart paper taped to the walls. One had the word "Cultivation" on it, while another had a rough drawing of a young plant with its roots stretching into the soil. Three other charts were blank.

"Looks like someone is getting in touch with his inner gardener again," Jerome said with a laugh. "Are you sure being a division manager is the right career choice for you?"

"Hey," David replied with a sarcastic look. "Stop trying to be a 'weed' in my team meeting."

As the meeting was about to begin, David noticed that Chris was absent and made a mental note to check on him later. After taking care of a few administrative details, David began explaining the papers on the walls.

"A few weeks ago, we talked about *what* we want to grow as a team. Today I want our discussion to be more about *how* we grow them."

David introduced the idea of cultivation and how he saw it as a strategy for improvement and accelerating growth.

"If you frequently check the condition of plants, you're going to see what those plants need to grow. You're going to notice any weeds or that the plants lack sufficient water. You're going to help them grow at an optimum rate.

"Today I want us to practice some of our own cultivation," David continued. "Let's see how we're doing on achieving our goals and determine what we might do to help our goals become reality even faster.

"The first way we practice cultivation," David began, "is by looking at our priorities to see if they're aligned with the goals and priorities of the organization."

They all seemed to be in agreement until Raj spoke up and said, "One place I see us at odds is with customer retention. Trendex wants us to make retention a priority, but as a division we seem to be focusing more on new customer acquisition."

"Thanks for that insight, Raj," David said, wishing Chris was there to hear his comment. His team's inability to keep quality technicians was a big reason why they were losing some customers.

After looking at some other areas where they were aligned or at odds with company priorities, David asked his team how they were aligning their individual work with the stated priorities of the division. He then moved to the second flipchart and wrote "Processes."

"Another place we need to look to ensure we're growing the right things," David stated, "is at our processes – how we go about our work each day as individuals and as a division."

Felicia eagerly spoke up and said, "I've got an idea for this one. As a division, we constantly talk about how we want more time to focus on our top priorities. But then I have to spend at least an hour each week completing a status report that has information people could easily access through our company's internal databases."

Jerome joined the conversation. "I agree," he said. "We share most of that information in our weekly meetings anyway. It seems like an inefficient use of our time, especially with all we are expected to make happen."

David wrote "status reports" on the "Processes" list as they continued their discussion of other ways work gets done and communication is shared. While many of the suggestions required further research by David, at least he had a better understanding of their challenges.

Pleased with their progress so far, David headed to the final flipchart and wrote "People" at the top.

"While priorities and processes may include things related to how we work together," David said, "I think we also need to spend some time specifically focusing on what we can do to help grow *each other*. It goes back to the four questions I ask each of you from time to time:

- What environment will help you deliver your best work?

- What else do you need to deliver your best work?

- What do you see as the most limiting factor to delivering your best work?

- What motivates you to deliver your best work?

Keith was the first to speak up this time. "David, as the 'old guy' on the team," he said, "I appreciate all the work you're trying to do to help us. One thing I'd like to see is for us to have an environment where people's ideas and abilities are more highly respected."

David nodded uncertainly. "Okay... could you be a little more specific?" he asked.

"Sure," Keith replied. "I came to you with a suggestion on how we could better teach new technicians our troubleshooting methodology several weeks ago. I haven't heard anything since."

"I'm sorry, Keith," David said. "I've just been so busy working on other things."

"I know," Keith replied, "and I respect that. What you *could* have done is let me do some exploratory work or even design a training model. That would have made it easier for you to say yes or no to moving forward and showed me that you value my ideas and my ability to follow through with them."

Keith's words were right on target. David recognized that he had been trying to make sure everything was done just right and wasn't using the resources on his team wisely. It was time to get more serious about growing his team.

Smiling at Keith, David said, "I agree. I need to be more intentional about growing each of you. And that can only happen if I give you more responsibility. Stick around after we're done with this meeting, and we'll talk about next steps."

With that suggestion handled, David fielded some other thoughts from the group, thanked them for sharing their insights and concluded the meeting.

After his side meeting with Keith, David went looking for Chris. If he had been in the meeting, he would have heard Raj's comments and maybe felt a greater sense of urgency to change. Even with David telling him what Raj said, Chris might see it as David's way of questioning his ability to manage his team.

Arriving at Chris's office, David saw him on the phone and waited outside for a moment. Chris motioned for him to come in as he was finishing up his call. Chris spoke first.

"Hey, David," Chris began. "Sorry I missed the meeting. Man, I've been on the phone with a customer for almost two hours. Let me tell you, they are not pleased."

"What's wrong?" David asked.

"Oh, they aren't happy with one of the technicians I sent out there last week," Chris replied. "I keep telling them that you can't find good help anymore and that we're doing the best we can."

Chris's comments enraged David. He hoped that Chris didn't detect his change in color as he listened. While David wanted to start dissecting all that was wrong with what Chris had told the customer, he decided to try a different approach.

"Chris," David began, "I certainly understand that emergencies happen, and I hate that you missed the meeting today. Any chance you and I could take a few minutes now to go over what you missed?"

"Sure," Chris replied.

"Great," David said. "It's a nice day. Why don't we find a table outside in the break area? Sounds like both of us could use some fresh air."

Finding a table and sitting down, David reviewed the idea of cultivation with Chris and briefly discussed the "3Ps" of Priorities, Processes and People.

"So the way I see it, Chris," David said, "one way for us to improve as a division and individually is to consistently address these three areas."

Chris glanced at the paper in front of him and said, "Makes sense."

"Good," David replied. "To make sure I've explained it well, let's apply it to what's going on in your world. Let's look at priorities for a moment." David reminded Chris of Trendex's priority of retaining more current customers.

David asked, "Chris, if I judged your priorities by what you said on that last customer phone call, would it be fair to say that your priority was a little different?"

"But you weren't there for the whole conversation, David," Chris shot back.

"I know, I know," David replied. "That's a fair statement. I just want to show you that sometimes we might *say* we understand the priorities of the company but not actually align our own priorities with them."

Chris seemed to want to say more but just nodded in mild agreement instead.

David then moved on to processes and asked, "Chris, do you see any processes in our company that might be limiting your ability to retain more of our current customers?"

"Absolutely," Chris replied without missing a beat. "Because of some changes in how we hire at Trendex, I'm not getting the quality of applicants I need to fill these positions."

Happy to see Chris more fully engaged in the conversation, he spent the next few minutes talking about some changes that would help him find better-qualified technicians. And he also had a suggestion of his own.

"Chris, do you ever go out on service calls with your new hires?" David asked.

"Rarely," Chris replied. "I normally leave that up to one of the lead technicians. If there's a problem, they contact me."

"Hmmm," David mused. "I wonder…"

"Wonder what?" Chris inquired.

"I wonder if you might get a better understanding of what you need from your new technicians if you saw some of their struggles first-hand," David replied. "And then maybe you could work with HR to determine how to find people with more of the skills you need them to have when they're first hired."

"Maybe," Chris said. "But who has the time?"

"Funny you should mention that," David said. "In our meeting today, we looked at a few things that, if changed, might free you up for a couple hours a week. Would that be enough?"

"I think so," Chris replied. "We have some customers in the local area."

"Perfect," David said. "Let me see what I can do about finding you that time."

David then moved on to the third P: people. After reiterating the four key questions he had already asked, Chris chimed in and said, "Well, I've got one for your 'What do you need to deliver your best work?' category."

"Okay," David replied. "Let me have it."

"My technicians work hard, and I know they don't always deliver stellar performance, but they're trying," Chris began. "It would be nice to have more of the 'higher ups' have something positive to say about their efforts every now and then. The only time we ever hear from them is when something goes wrong."

Like Keith's earlier comments, Chris's words rang true. While he would like to blame those he reported to, David knew that part of the blame lay with him. In his push to make things better in the division, he had neglected to acknowledge and appreciate what was good. He put his pen down and looked squarely at Chris.

"Chris, you're right, and I take full responsibility for the oversight," David said. "Your team probably sees more of what's really going on with our customers than most of us do. We need to do a better job of supporting your efforts and listening to what you have to say. I guess I'll add that to my list of 'processes' I need to change in the way I lead."

Chris was visibly moved. David was the first manager who really took the time to understand his situation… and acknowledge that he didn't have all the answers.

As they got up to return to their offices, Chris looked at David and said, "Thanks, David. It means a lot to me that you didn't just lecture me about how I should be talking to customers differently. You took the time to show me how to improve, and I'm grateful. Maybe your 'growing mindset' for leaders *isn't* just another passing fad."

"Thanks, Chris. I appreciate the vote of confidence," David said with an affirming nod.

CUTTING BACK TO GROW FORWARD

David next visited Kelly in late November. He wasn't exactly sure what they would be doing since the growing season was over, and the retail store would be the only area in operation.

Driving to Kelly's place, David reflected on how far he had come with his division. They were on the verge of their most successful quarter in two years. Keith was still there but talking more and more about retirement. Chris was more excited than ever because his technicians had the most improved customer satisfaction scores of all divisions in the country... and the executive VP called him to express his gratitude.

All of this success, however, had not come without a price. Jerome left, and Jordan, his replacement, was taking more time to get up to speed than he had planned. Felicia and Liam were showing signs of fatigue from the frantic pace of the past few months, and he was afraid he might lose them to opportunities that weren't so demanding or draining.

Reflecting on Kelly's success in her business, David wondered if she had any ideas about how he could reduce the strain on his team while also helping them continue to excel.

As he walked toward Kelly's office, David noticed she was on the phone, so he took a seat at her conference table. She finished up her call and sat down next to David.

"Good to see you, sis," David said.

"You, too, David," Kelly replied.

David noticed the wistful nature in her voice and said, "What's wrong? You aren't your normal chipper self today."

Kelly took a deep breath and regained her composure. "Oh, I just got off the phone with a produce wholesaler. They had heard about my success growing an heirloom tomato and asked if I would be willing to start producing a large number of tomatoes for them. The amount of money they're willing to pay is pretty incredible."

"Congratulations, Kelly," David said. "What great news!"

"Maybe... but I had to turn him down," Kelly replied.

"Why?" David asked.

"My primary purpose in growing those heirloom tomatoes is for my local customers," Kelly answered, shifting some papers on the table. "I'm just not ready to make that much of a major adjustment in my business plan right now. I decided it was much better to tell him no now than to create havoc for myself and my team later."

"In other words," David replied, "you had to say no to something so you could say yes to something else."

"Almost correct," Kelly replied. "Being a commercial grower has taught me that **you sometimes have to say no to things of lesser importance so you can say yes to things of greater importance**. I could spend my time and energy on a thousand different things, but I wouldn't grow anything well."

As David reflected on her words, Kelly stood up and said, "In fact, I think I can give you a pretty good visual of what I'm talking about while we work today."

"Work?" David replied. "I thought work was over for the season. The apples have been harvested, the vegetables have been sold, and the weather is getting colder. What else is there to do?"

You sometimes have to say no to things of lesser importance so you can say yes to things of greater importance.

"You still aren't getting the full picture, are you?" Kelly sighed. She pointed to the quote on the bulletin board: *You are always a gardener. What grows – and how it grows – is up to you.*

"Every day, I have the opportunity to take actions that will move me closer to the results I want – or move me farther away," Kelly explained. "I choose the former, so we need to get to work."

David gave Kelly one of those 'you win but I don't like it' looks and followed her out of the office.

They got into a truck and headed to one of the orchards. Kelly rummaged around in the back of the truck once they arrived.

"Here, hold this," she said as she handed him a three-foot stepladder and a pair of pruning shears. She got the same items for herself, and they walked to the rows of trees in front of them.

"Today we're pruning," Kelly announced as she set her ladder down.

"Finally! Something I can understand," David said as he moved around to the other side of the first tree. "How much do you want me to cut off the top?" Kelly quickly seized his arm. "It's not quite that easy. Maybe on a hedge in a landscape, but not in my world," Kelly responded as she turned back to the truck. "Let me draw it out for you." She took a pad and pencil out of the truck and sketched a tree.

"We have to start by asking what we want the tree to look like two to three years from now," she explained. "In the case of apple trees, we want to create a tree with five to six main limbs, or stems, growing up. From these limbs will grow smaller limbs that ultimately produce the apples."

Beginning to sense the complexity of this type of pruning, David asked, "Why couldn't you just wait until summer to prune?

"If we prune in the summer," Kelly responded, "We would waste some of the tree's resources because we'd be cutting off something the tree has attempted to grow. Pruning now helps ensure that the tree's resources are being used more efficiently now to create the desired results later."

"You mean the best apples?" David asked.

"Exactly," Kelly responded. "**Pruning is a reallocation of resources to nurture the desired growth**." Putting her notepad back in the truck, she picked up her ladder and shears.

"Now, do you think you're ready to learn about how to prune apple trees?" Kelly asked.

"Yes, but don't blame me if you're broke in a few years because you let me help you," David replied.

Pruning is a reallocation of resources to nurture the desired growth.

Kelly began: "Remember the conversation we had in the office about growing more heirloom tomatoes and my saying no? Let's apply the same reasoning to this tree. How many main limbs or branches do you see?"

David stood back for a moment and said, "Six, I think."

"Right," Kelly said, "but look over here." She put her hand on a small limb that seemed of little significance to David. "What about this limb? Do you think I need to cut it off?"

"Not really," David replied. "It doesn't seem to be in the way or trying to compete with the other limbs."

"It may not be *now*," Kelly replied, "but what about as it grows in one, two or even three years from now?"

David saw her point and said, "It could be a problem."

"Yes, and what's the advantage of cutting it off now?" Kelly asked.

David thought for a moment and said, "So we don't waste the resources of the tree on something we really don't want."

"Perfect!" Kelly responded. "Now go back to what I was struggling with in the office. Maybe growing those heirloom tomatoes didn't seem like a lot of extra work now, but in the spring it would have required more and more effort on my part. The larger I let producing them become, the more it would have drawn away resources needed for my core business.

"By saying no *now*," she continued. "I minimize the chances of creating an undesirable result *later*. It wasn't an easy decision, because the additional income in the short term would be helpful. I just knew it was best for what I'm trying to grow here."

"So the key to knowing how and what to prune is being able to envision what you want the results to be in the future, after the tree has grown," David stated.

"Right!" Kelly responded. "**Pruning frees up resources that can be used in the areas of greatest importance.**"

They looked at a couple of other trees, and then Kelly began the actual pruning process with some members of her team. As she worked, David frequently drew parallels between his own situation and the trees in front of him.

Pruning frees up resources that can be used in the areas of greatest importance.

At work, he sometimes allowed himself and his team to spend too much time on projects that should have been stopped. He also was guilty of saying yes to too many things and, while they didn't seem like "big limbs" at the time, they had grown to the point where they were taking resources away from areas he knew were more important. He could have saved himself a lot of stress and frustration if he had pruned them earlier.

The sound of footsteps shook him from his time of reflection.

"Your turn, David," Kelly began. "We all need to practice a little pruning every now and then."

David tentatively took the pruning shears from Kelly and walked to one of the trees. Even though he thought he had the hang of it, Kelly still had to stop him from making inappropriate cuts from time to time.

"Not as easy as it looks, huh?" Kelly said, thinking back to David's oversimplified ideas about pruning. "Let's stop with this row. Ryan and the others will finish up later."

David picked up his ladder, and they loaded the items back into the truck. As they drove toward the office, David thought about all he had learned – but he still had one question to ask Kelly about pruning.

PRUNING TIPS

- You sometimes have to say no to things of lesser importance so you can say yes to things of greater importance.

- Pruning is a reallocation of resources to nurture the desired growth.

- Pruning frees up resources that can be used in the areas of greatest importance.

LEARNING THAT
TIMING IS EVERYTHING

As Kelly drove past an area of the orchard with older trees, David asked her to stop. As she pulled the truck to the side of the gravel road, David asked, "Is pruning done the same way with these older trees as the younger ones?"

"Why do you ask?"

"Well," David replied, "I see how important it is to keep the younger trees pruned to encourage one type of growth and discourage another type, but it would seem that if they've been pruned correctly in the early years, the amount of pruning needed as they grew older would be less."

"Sure," Kelly replied. "**Pruning is *most* critical in the early stages of growth because you're forming the structure for the future.** If we have done our job correctly, most of our future pruning is spent on removing the dead, damaged, deformed or diseased branches."

"So pruning at the right time is crucial, huh?" David asked.

Pruning is *most* critical in the early stages of growth because you're forming the structure for the future.

"Yes," Kelly said. "Timing is vital when resources are limited. Timing also is one of the hardest things to teach people. There's one key principle about pruning that if they ever internalize, they're much more effective at growing anything well."

"What is that?" David asked.

"It's really rather simple," Kelly replied. "**Prune at the first signs of undesirable outcomes**. I can't tell you the number of times I've walked through one of the orchards and noticed several trees in need of some minor pruning. The manager will tell me that they will 'get to it' in a few days.

"On our next review," she continued, "I'll see those same trees with larger limbs that now need major pruning. When I ask why they haven't taken care of it, they say they were 'just too busy.' It's then that I remind them that their trees aren't growing in an acceptable way."

David immediately connected with Kelly's comment about "the first signs of undesirable outcomes." He knew he had been pushing Jerome too hard. Jerome had even said to David on a number of occasions, "You keep adding things to my plate, but you never take anything away." David realized that his failure to prune Jerome's workload had cost him a valuable member of his team.

David chuckled as they moved back toward the truck. "Where were you about three years ago when I needed this lesson on pruning?" he asked.

"How so?" Kelly asked.

Prune at the first signs of undesirable outcomes.

"Well," David began, "I had taken on way too many things at one time. I had accepted three new clients that took up a lot of my time. Emma was only 2, and Amy was overwhelmed between her teaching schedule and keeping things functioning at the house. I also was the coach for Ashley's soccer team.

"Mom, as you well know, was in failing health and, if that wasn't enough, I accepted the lead role in raising money for a new community park. In gardening terms, I was trying to grow apples, kiwi, grapes, pecans and strawberries all at the same time."

"What would you have done differently, knowing what you know now?" Kelly asked.

"For starters," David began, "I would have paid more attention to how my situation was growing out of control and needed some pruning. I ignored those 'first signs' you mentioned such as more frequent arguments with Amy and Ashley not asking me to do things with her anymore because I was always telling her no due to other commitments. I also started missing some deadlines at work.

"I also would have accepted a more limited role on the park committee and entrusted more people to take on some of the responsibilities," he continued. "Looking back on my situation at work, I would have gone to my boss and sought more guidance and assistance with the new clients. He would have appreciated that because it would have moved things along more quickly and probably achieved better results.

"And..." David's voice trailed off for a moment. He swallowed hard and said, "And that would have given me more opportunities to spend time with mom."

Kelly put her hand on David's hand for a moment as they pulled up to the office. "I just feel like that was a time when I wasn't doing anything well, and I still think about it," he said.

"David, you were a great son to mom and still are to dad," Kelly said softly. "You *know* that. And I know the relationship you have with Amy, Emma and Ashley. Maybe you did make some choices *then* that you regret now, but the positive thing is that you recognize some ways to improve so that you don't experience those same regrets in the future."

Kelly reassuringly patted his shoulder as they exited the truck and walked into the office. After a few more minutes of conversation, he gave her a hug and headed home. It was time for him to do some pruning of his own.

MORE PRUNING TIPS

- Pruning is *most* critical in the early stages of growth, because you're forming the structure for the future.
- Prune at the first signs of undesirable outcomes.

MAKING BETTER CHOICES

David hadn't expected his time with Kelly to be quite so emotionally heavy, but he knew it had once again been valuable in helping him sort through his own situation. While things weren't growing out of control like they were three years ago, he still knew that a little pruning was in order.

David needed to get more serious about helping his team manage its workload and cut out, or at least reduce, time spent on activities that weren't fully contributing to their priorities as a division.

After dinner, David shared with Amy what he had learned about the idea of pruning:

- Pruning is a reallocation of resources to nurture the desired growth.

- Pruning at the right time frees up resources than can be used in the areas of greatest importance.

- Pruning in the early stages of growth is most critical, because you're forming the structure for the future.

- Prune at the first signs of undesirable outcomes.

Before applying the principles at work, he wanted to explore how they might work for he and Amy as they struggled with an overloaded schedule. Looking over David's notes, they discussed some "desirable outcomes" they wanted as a couple and as a family. From there, they looked at ways they could prune some items in their schedule. One immediate way was to delay Emma's entry into playing soccer. They had been considering it, but the extra time spent at practices and games couldn't be justified right now.

Amy also brought up their time with technology. Between laptops, tablets, smartphones and TV, it seemed like they rarely spent time together disconnected from their devices. They decided to set up "technology-free" time in the evenings to encourage more quality time together.

Amy then mentioned the need to be more conscious about noticing undesirable outcomes.

"Give me an example," David replied.

"Okay," Amy began, "how about when you're at home and your phone 'dings,' and you immediately check it?"

David gave a guilty grin and then said, "But I don't do that *all* the time."

"No, but when you do check it so quickly, it's a sign to me that things are a little out of control for you at work," Amy responded.

"You're right," David replied.

They spent the next few minutes making a list of other indicators that some pruning might be needed in their schedules:

- Lack of time for each other
- No opportunities to engage in their personal interests
- Not nurturing relationships with friends
- Being less than patient with the children, especially about little things
- Always arriving late to functions or activities
- Frequently hearing the phrase, "You didn't tell me about that"

After their discussion, David took the first step in doing some pruning for himself. He decided to hire someone to build a treehouse for Ashley and Emma. He and Amy loved working on projects together, but with the weather, the girls' schedules and the holidays coming up, he knew having someone else take care of it would reduce his stress... and help him keep a promise he had made to Ashley and Emma.

Feeling a sense of relief, David hoped he could sustain his momentum to make the right cuts at work. What he didn't know, however, was that someone else was contemplating some pruning too.

ENCOURAGING DESIRABLE GROWTH

With his personal pruning taking shape, David turned his attention to work. In his planning time one morning, he reflected on his division's priorities and how he was working with his team to accomplish them.

As he started looking at what to prune, he was surprised to find many things he needed to cut were attitudes driving negative behaviors. He listed several things:

- Thinking I always have to have the answers
- Feeling like I'm too busy growing others to take time to grow my own skills as a leader
- Worrying about the merger's impact on my team (and ME!)
- Being afraid to turn more responsibility over to individual team members

David also started taking the time to look at his team's current workload. He decided to have each team member start logging the hours spent on various activities so he could evaluate where adjustments could be made. His planning would have continued if not for a knock at the door. It was Keith.

"Hello, Keith. Good to see you," he said. "What can I do for you?"

"If you have a minute, I need to talk with you about the timeline for my retirement," Keith replied. "I want to make sure it isn't disruptive to the team."

As they moved to the conference table, David thought, "Filling Keith's position in the next few months could certainly drain resources I need for other things." Remembering Kelly's tip about "pruning at the right time," David tried a different approach.

"Keith," David began, "I hate to break it to you, but losing someone of your caliber will always create disruption in a company. In fact, before we have that discussion, can I ask *you* something?"

"Of course," Keith answered.

"I'm in full support of your retirement," David said. "Goodness knows you've earned it. But you still seem to enjoy so much of what you do here. If you could sum up your reasons for retirement, what would they be?"

"Oh, I can sum it up in *four* words," Keith answered.

"Really?" David asked, puzzled. "What are they?"

"The pace of change!" Keith responded tersely. "I'm tired of always having to stay informed about a new product or learn a new software program."

David sat back in his chair and thought for a moment.

"So if I could reduce your stress related to change, you would consider staying?"

Keith looked off into the distance for a second and then said, "Yes, I think I would. I do love working here, and things have certainly gotten better under your leadership."

David thanked Keith for his compliment and said, "Give me a few days, and let's see if I can come up with a solution." Keith nodded in agreement.

After meeting with Keith, David went to Liam's office. He had an idea about how to help Keith. David knocked on his door, and Liam called out, "Come in."

David sat down and, after a few pleasantries, said, "How would you like to have a few more opportunities to work on some technology-related projects?"

"I'd love it," Liam responded, "but my plate is already full."

"I know," David said, "but I might be able to help with that, too."

David set a meeting date with Keith and Liam before returning to his office.

At the meeting a few days later, David was pleased to see how receptive Keith and Liam were to working together. It was almost comical. Keith would complain about something he had to do related to training others on technology or online tasks, and Liam would say, "Oh, that's easy." Then Liam would vent about why something had to be done a certain way, and Keith would give him the background and reasons for the policy or procedure.

When the meeting was over, David could see that he had made the right call – or "cuts" – in this situation. He was removing obstacles to the growth of both Keith and Liam.

"Maybe this team *can* pull it off," David thought. His team was growing like never before, but would it be enough to satisfy his vice president and the executive team?

Remembering Kelly's comment that gardeners have to focus on what they can control, he felt like he was doing everything he could to create a high-performing team. But he was wrong.

WATCHING IT GROW

Several months had passed since David's pruning session with Kelly. As he drove along the highway, David reflected on some recent "wins:"

- His idea of quantifying the time needed for almost every activity or assignment had helped his team distribute the workload more evenly.

- Because he worked to consistently create a safe environment for his team, he was always being given ideas on how they could improve their work.

- Keith's comment several months earlier about how he should give more responsibility and authority to his team led David to delegate much more effectively.

- A more significant part of his day was now spent thinking and working strategically instead of responding to crises.

Arriving at Kelly's place, he came upon a flurry of activity. Workers on forklifts were unloading large wooden crates of apples and moving them into the processing area. Once the apples rolled onto the conveyor belt, they were washed, graded and bagged or boxed for sale. Other workers loaded large trucks with the finished product for delivery to surrounding farmers' markets, produce stands and retail stores.

David parked at the far end of the parking lot so as not to be in the way of customers and trucks. He walked into the store and was greeted by even more activity. He found Kelly over by a stand of apples, talking to a customer. She motioned for him to join them.

"Linda," Kelly began, "I want you to meet my brother, David. David, this is Linda. She's been buying apples here for over 20 years."

"Pleased to meet you," David replied.

"Same here," Linda responded. "Your sister can sure grow some amazing apples."

"Yes, she definitely knows how to win the blue ribbons in that category," David responded, pointing to large red and yellow apples on display. Kelly smiled and nodded her head in gratitude.

"Thanks for stopping in, Linda," Kelly said. "I look forward to seeing you again." David smiled at Linda as he and Kelly walked outside.

"Wow!" David said. "This is incredible. I don't think I've ever seen it this busy around here."

"Well," Kelly responded. "You just haven't been here during harvest season. Let's head up to the orchard for a few minutes. I need some time away, and it will give us a chance to catch up."

David and Kelly got into the truck and headed toward the orchards. The fresh air and scent of ripening apples were just the respite David needed from the hectic pace of the past few months.

Returning his attention to Kelly, he asked, "How profitable do you think this year's crop will be for you?"

"Not sure yet," Kelly replied. "And to be honest, that's not the most important thing right now."

David was taken aback by her answer.

"Sure it is," he said. "If you don't make a profit, you're out of business."

"True," Kelly said, "but it's not the *only* thing. **The harvest is about much more than the numbers**. There are some years when our profit margins have been really small, but other elements of our harvest have been really large."

"You've lost me now," David said. "Maybe you *do* need me to come help run your business."

Kelly smirked and said sarcastically, "Like that would work."

The harvest is about much more than the numbers.

They both laughed, and Kelly continued. "Let me show you what I mean."

They stopped the truck where yellow apples were being picked and loaded into crates.

"What do you see out there?" Kelly asked.

"I see some people working really hard picking apples."

"That's only part of the picture," Kelly responded. "I also see three guys who came to work for me two years ago and didn't have a clue what they wanted to do with their lives. I gave them a chance to work, and now they're supervisors for their respective crews.

"That's an outcome I need to celebrate," she continued. "It might not impact my bottom line in a major way this year, but it certainly *is* one of the reasons we're experiencing success. To me, **harvest is when you celebrate *all* of your productive results**."

Harvest is when you celebrate *all* of your productive results.

David thought back to a conversation with Chris several months ago and his revelation that he needed to praise his team members more for what they were doing well at that moment. He hadn't considered their small achievements part of the team's "harvest," but he understood now that it was important.

Sensing David's pessimism, Kelly said, "Let's look at it another way. Think about Linda, the lady you met a few minutes ago. What's the value in having a customer who's been buying from me for 20 years? Sure, she may only buy a bushel of apples or a few strawberries each year, but I need to celebrate the fact that I grow a quality product people want to buy – and that I have someone telling others about their positive experiences here."

They drove to another part of the orchard where crews were picking apples and joined the group. David grabbed one of the cloth bags, placed it over his shoulder, climbed a ladder and began picking.

He was lost in thought about Kelly's comments – *harvest is when you celebrate all of your productive results.* He was a little disappointed in himself for not having a "harvest" attitude more often. He frequently beat himself up for his team not meeting its goals. He rarely took the time to look at what he (or they) *were* doing well. He now realized that not celebrating the small wins with his team was not only hurting his own motivation, but it also was limiting his team's desire to focus on its goals.

David stepped down from the ladder and unloaded his bag of apples into one of the wooden crates. Kelly came over to join him, and they started working on another tree.

"Sorry I wasn't here to help with that last tree," she said. "I was talking with one of the workers about the new addition to his family."

"That's okay, Kelly," David responded. "I'd imagine you consider *that* part of your harvest as well."

"Absolutely!" she replied. "I believe people bring their hearts *and* minds to work, and I want to connect with them in both places. It's another thing I absolutely love about my job."

Her comments made David think about his own job situation. "Speaking of jobs, I may need to join you soon if things don't go our way in the merger."

"The official announcement is coming up soon?" Kelly asked as she scaled her ladder.

"Yes, and I just don't know if we've done enough to satisfy the executive team overseeing the whole thing," David replied. "That would be the harvest for us."

"Well, there's a way to find out if you've done enough," Kelly responded.

"I know... If I still have a division to lead after the announcement," David said.

"No, I mean *right now*," Kelly answered.

"What? How? Is the altitude getting to you on that ladder?" David jeered.

"Maybe, but I'm not the one worried about having to go to work for his sister," Kelly retorted.

"Okay," David replied. "Let's hear it."

Kelly began. "You already know my favorite quote: *You are always a gardener. What grows – and how it grows – is up to you.* For years, that one phrase helped me be intentional about what I worked on every day – primarily building this business.

"But I soon began to notice that just focusing on the growing side of things blinded me to what I was actually achieving, or 'harvesting' – strong relationships with others, good health, financial security and service to the community. As a gardener, I've come to realize the need to **reflect on the results of your *efforts* rather than just on what you're trying to grow.**"

> ## Reflect on the results of your *efforts* rather than just on what you're trying to grow.

"So how does that help me know if I've done everything to be successful with my team?" David asked.

"Well," Kelly replied, "I typically ask myself three questions:

- What did I do to create the environment for the right things to grow?
- What steps did I take to help the right things grow well?
- What did I do to ensure that resources were being utilized to nurture the desired growth?

When I have specific answers to those three questions, I consider myself a successful grower, regardless of what my physical harvest turns out to be."

David thought for a moment as he was getting off the ladder. "It goes back to being intentional, doesn't it?" he asked.

"Sure does," Kelly responded. "**You have to be intentional about celebrating your harvest *moments* as well as focusing on what you're trying to grow.**"

David and Kelly picked the last apples from the tree and placed them in the crate. "Isn't it about lunchtime?" David asked.

You have to be intentional about celebrating your harvest *moments* as well as focusing on what you're trying to grow.

"You're surrounded by some of the tastiest apples in the world," Kelly answered. "What could be better than that?"

David laughed as he picked an apple out of the crate and got into the truck. "I'll consider this my '*apple*tizer,'" he said.

Kelly rolled her eyes as they drove back toward the office. Still snickering, David crunched into the juicy red apple.

After grabbing their sandwiches out of Kelly's office and stopping for a few minutes for Kelly to talk with some customers, they walked out behind the old barn and sat down at a picnic table.

"If I understand this growing mindset correctly, I think you're telling me that effort should be celebrated, not just achievement," David said.

"You bet," Kelly replied. "I've had years where my team and I worked really hard to grow the right things, but because of the weather or the economy or something else out of our control, we just didn't get the results we needed. That doesn't mean the individuals and the effort they put forth shouldn't be celebrated in some way."

Even though Kelly was talking about her work team, David recognized the correlation with his family. They had always found great joy in helping elderly people around their community by preparing meals or completing household chores for them. Other times, they picked flowers and made simple arrangements to brighten someone's day. Emma often designed cards with her own personal drawings, and Ashley would sometimes play her violin for residents at the local nursing home.

With their crazy schedules during the past few months, David and his family had not been as disciplined with their acts of kindness as he thought they should be. He had even expressed disappointment to his family on several occasions. Hearing Kelly's comments reminded him that as someone responsible for the growth of his family, he should be praising more of what they *were* doing instead of frequently expressing concern over what they were *not* doing.

After they finished lunch, Kelly walked with David to his car. "There's another question I ask myself from time to time that helps me evaluate my progress."

"What's that?" David replied.

"I ask myself, 'Am I a better gardener than I was a year ago?'"

"Oh," David said brightly. "That's a good one. I'll have to think about that on my way home. Thanks for all of the advice, Kelly."

David gave one last wave and closed the door.

On the drive home, Kelly's question kept tugging at him... "Are you a better gardener than you were a year ago?"

David reflected on his time as a division manager. There was no doubt his team was more fully engaged on the division's priorities and getting close to meeting its goals. He smiled as he thought about the individual growth of each team member. "Even Chris is getting his hands dirty," David chuckled as he thought about how Chris had improved as a manager under his leadership.

Thinking of his family, David knew his relationship with Amy had improved since he had become more intentional about taking care of her needs and working to create an environment where time with her and the girls was a consistent priority. "That reminds me," David thought. "I've got to start planning our anniversary trip."

As his attention shifted to how he had improved his personal leadership style, he thought about how he was much more willing to ask for help. Any time he needed to address a complex problem or explore a new area of leadership, he would jokingly say to himself, "I'll bet there's a mentor or a coach for that." And he would start looking for the right person.

With all of these positive thoughts swirling in his head, David said to himself, "Kelly's right. I need to celebrate more of the things I *have* accomplished instead of focusing on the two or three things I *haven't* accomplished."

David decided that regardless of the uncertainty the next few weeks would bring, he needed to help his team recognize how far they had come.

HARVESTING TIPS

- The harvest is about much more than the numbers.
- Harvest is when you celebrate *all* of your productive results.
- Reflect on the results of your *efforts* rather than just on what you're trying to grow.
- You have to be intentional about celebrating your harvest *moments* as well as focusing on what you're trying to grow.

RIPENING FAST

With his new focus on "harvest moments," David decided to get his team together outside of the office for a celebration. He thought about a local conference center and even entertained the idea of having everyone over to his house, but the more he thought about it, there was only one place that would be perfect... Kelly's Place!

After calling Kelly to get her approval, David scheduled the date, reserved a company van and began planning the afternoon's activities.

"Welcome to our harvest celebration!" David said as the team loaded into the van on the day of the trip.

Liam, never one to hold back and also thinking about the merger, spoke up and said, "Don't you mean our possible going away party?"

David quickly responded with, "No. If we need to have one of those in a few weeks, we can do that, too. What I want this afternoon to be is a celebration of the results we've achieved so far." He started the engine and headed toward the interstate.

When they arrived, Kelly greeted them in the parking lot, and David introduced her to everyone on his team. They began the afternoon by touring the greenhouse and retail center. Kelly was amazed at all they remembered from David's conversations with them about growing plants. With this part of the tour over, they got back in the van and headed up to the apple orchards.

After a quick drive along a field of young apple trees, David stopped in a place with a panoramic view of the surrounding hills. Kelly had set a table with water, apple cider and an assortment of desserts, including apple crumble. Once everyone got a plate and was seated, David spoke up.

"As I said before we left, I want this to be a time of celebration. At work, we get so caught up in checking off the next item on our list that we don't take time to stop and reflect on what we've accomplished as a team."

David then brought out a flipchart with three questions:

- What have I done to create an environment where the right things can grow for our division?
- What steps have I taken to help the right things grow well?
- What have I done to ensure that resources are being utilized to nurture the desired growth?

David gave his answers to the questions and then invited others to respond.

Answers were slow at first but, as people became comfortable with the exercise, the responses flowed more freely.

Chris's celebration was how he had transformed the hiring process for his technicians. For Keith, it was pruning his poor attitude about technology and how that allowed him to appreciate and work more effectively with Liam.

Raj said his win was that he had been partly responsible for reducing the division's operating costs by six percent. As a new hire, Jordan said his greatest contribution so far was not making a mistake. The team laughed as Liam said, "Then you're not doing your job!"

Felicia was the last to offer her thoughts.

"For me," she began, "my biggest contribution has been making sure our best ideas were given a chance to come to fruition. It was so frustrating in previous companies when you would work so hard to develop a new idea, only to be told you had to stop before you saw any real results."

David made a few final comments and finished by saying, "Regardless of what next week's announcement brings, I want you to know that, in my mind, you are all 'master gardeners.' Whether we have a week or a decade left together, I couldn't let another day go by without telling you and saying thanks."

After a few more trips to the dessert table and soaking in the beautiful scenery, the group returned to the van.

When they made a quick stop at the retail center on the way out, David saw Chris looking over the "Growers of Tomorrow" wall. He walked over to him and said, "Interesting concept, huh?"

"Yes it is," Chris replied casually. "In fact, we might need to put *your* picture up there soon."

David laughed and said, "Yeah, right. Just because I've learned how to use Kelly's principles to be a stronger leader doesn't mean I can do what some of these people have done."

Chris turned and said, "Don't be so sure."

"What do you mean?" David asked, now thoroughly intrigued by Chris's comment.

Chris took a deep breath. "Well, I didn't want to say anything with all the 'merger swirl' going on right now, but I might be leaving the team."

"I hate to hear that, Chris," David said. "I know our time together didn't start out perfect, but I'd like to think we've learned a lot from each other."

"Exactly," Chris said. "And that's why I might be leaving. Our central division manager is retiring, and I've been encouraged to apply for the position."

"Wonderful!" David said.

"It's because of you, David," Chris said with a more assertive tone. "You're the one who made it possible. You're the first division manager I've had who didn't see me as a problem. You took the time to really get to know me and what I could contribute to the team. You went out of your way to make sure I had what I needed to be successful. And now others outside our division are noticing my accomplishments. I don't know how to thank you."

David paused for a moment, glanced around the room and then said, "I do."

"How?" Chris asked.

"Lead that division in such a way that *your* picture should be on this wall one day," David replied.

Chris smiled and said, "If I get the chance, I'll do my best."

They walked to the van and headed back to Trendex.

REAPING THE REWARDS?

The trip to Kelly's place had done much to boost morale, but there was no denying that people were still feeling anxious about the pending announcement.

David tried to keep things moving along as normal. In their weekly team meeting, he intentionally brought up some elements of their three-year strategic plan so they would look beyond the week. The last thing he wanted was for them to take things this far and then let up at the end. "We have to keep growing," he thought to himself.

David spent some time reviewing his notes from his visits with Kelly. He had learned so much about being a leader through her "growing" mindset. From creating the right environment to having a consistent routine and removing obstacles to growth, David felt more confident than ever. More important, he had developed a leadership model that was helping him succeed in other areas of his life, regardless of the merger outcome.

The formal announcement about the merger would be made on Friday, but David's vice president wanted to personally give him the news about his division on Thursday. Walking into the building on Thursday morning, David was surprised to see all of his team members' offices empty. "A possible sign of things to come," he thought to himself.

A few minutes later, Raj was in David's office when the phone rang. When the name "Brett Wilson" appeared on caller ID, he knew he needed to take the call. Brett was the vice president over his division. He picked up the handset.

"Good morning, Brett Wilson," David said.

"Good morning, David," Brett replied. After a couple of superficial comments, Brett got to the point. "David, I'd like to talk with you about the impact of the merger on your division."

"Sure," came David's reply. "What works for you?"

"Come on up in about 30 minutes," Brett answered. "I'll see you then."

David hung up the phone and mentioned the meeting to Raj as they finished their discussion. While the meeting wasn't a surprise, David felt the anxiety building. The numbers didn't lie. The company Trendex was merging with had a division almost identical to the one David was managing, and it had a strong history of success. With time, David knew his division could put up more impressive numbers, but there was no pruning, cultivating or pixie dust that would get them there more quickly.

Walking out of his office and up the stairs, he tried to relax. "Well, at least if I lose my job at Trendex, I can go work for Kelly," he thought. But the joke did little to calm his nerves.

He turned left off the stairs and let Brett's assistant know he was there for the meeting. She told him to go on in. He took a deep breath as he opened the door.

To his surprise, David wasn't the only one invited to the meeting. In the room was his entire team: Keith, Chris, Liam, Felicia, Jordan and Raj. David's fears were now at full throttle because he knew the outcome of the merger: his division was being cut. David appreciated that Brett didn't leave him to tell his team members on his own, but he would have liked a little more notice. Shaking hands with Brett and acknowledging the others, David took a seat.

Brett began: "I appreciate all of you taking time to meet with me today. I'll keep this brief, because I realize you all have a lot going on. As you know, a lot of research and study has been done to determine the best course of action to take with the merger. As the vice president overseeing this division, I'm grateful that David was willing to serve as division manager during such an uncertain time. That's not easy."

David could feel his face reddening; he looked around the room and saw similar expressions.

Brett continued: "At this point, the executive team overseeing the merger…"

Before he could finish, David interrupted and said, "Brett, may I say something first?"

"Sure, David."

"These are fantastic people," David said. "The longer I work with them, the more I appreciate their willingness to tackle difficult assignments. We've come so far together. They just needed more time and a better leader."

"That's very noble, David," Brett responded, "but I think you need to give some credit to your team members for the – what's the word – 'harvest' you're experiencing."

"Harvest? Yes, of course, but..." David struggled to make sense of what Brett had just said. "Aren't you going to…"

Brett finished David's statement: "…cut your division?"

"Yes…," David replied feebly.

"No, we're not!" Brett answered. His team members began laughing and clapping.

"We finally pulled one over on YOU, David," Liam yelled.

"Yeah," Raj answered. "I was glad Brett got to the point. I thought you were going to pass out on us."

David exhaled and lowered his head, overwhelmed by the moment.

"My purpose today," Brett continued, "is to congratulate all of you on your extraordinary efforts. You've worked under a tremendous amount of stress for quite a while, and I'm thrilled to see how things have turned around. In fact, I was so interested in how you accomplished it that I went straight to the experts for the answers."

Brett got up and walked to a flipchart in the corner of the room. Turning back the first page, he revealed a page with four words, each written near a corner of the page: "Growing," "Cultivating," "Pruning" and finally, "Harvesting." In the center of the page was the word "Always."

"But how did you know about...?" David asked.

"Let's just say I had a meeting with some pretty amazing gardeners this morning," Brett replied as he looked at David's team members.

Now it all made sense to him! The offices were empty earlier because they were all meeting with Brett.

David made eye contact with Raj. "YOU!" he said. "You were in my office and didn't mention a thing about it."

Raj simply smiled and said, "And miss the moment we just had? The look on your face was priceless."

David shook his head in disbelief. They had done it!

Brett continued the meeting, giving some additional feedback from the executive team and again congratulating them on their achievements.

After a flurry of celebratory handshakes and hugs, they all headed back to their offices.

Taking a moment for himself, David walked down the steps and out the front door of the building and took a deep breath. "Yes!" he thought. "This is what being a strong leader feels like."

He called Amy to share the news. She was thrilled. "Sounds like someone owes a phone call to his sister," she said jokingly as they finished their conversation.

"She's next on my list," said David.

"Well hello, little brother!" Kelly answered. "Are you calling to apply for a job?"

David replied, "As tempting as that sounds, I think I'll just stay here and run this division of Trendex."

Kelly gave out a yell and said, "We'll miss you as an employee but look forward to seeing you as cheap labor every now and then."

David couldn't resist having a little fun with Kelly as he teased, "I think I've learned all I need to know about being a leader. I'm not sure I need to keep coming out to see you. That's a long drive and, with the merger, I've got more to do than ever."

Kelly broke the silence. "Well, speaking as a seasoned gardener, I would say that you still have a lot to learn. If Trendex thinks you've been successful with what you know *now*, just think of what you could do for that division if you had more lessons over the next few years."

"Well, if you're offering to continue the lessons," David replied, "I might be able to find a way to get there from time to time, especially if you have some of that world-famous apple crumble waiting for me."

"It's a deal, David," Kelly replied. "Now if you'll excuse me, I need to get back to the simple and carefree world of growing plants."

"Ha!" David replied. "I know better than that now. Thanks again, Kelly."

David ended the call and headed up to his office. And this time there was no question about how long he would be there.

A NEW GROWING SEASON

Several years had passed since David experienced his first growing season as a leader at Trendex, but it certainly wasn't the last. He received several additional promotions, and he was always careful to evaluate new opportunities against how they would affect his family as well as his own personal well-being. *"You are always a gardener. What grows – and how it grows – is up to you"* had become his guiding philosophy.

During David's tenure at Trendex, they established a "Growers of Tomorrow" award that recognized managers and directors who were instrumental in helping their direct reports grow their leadership skills.

Ashley had finished college and was now working as a music therapist. Having spent a considerable amount of time with her Aunt Kelly, Emma became interested in plants and gardening and was looking forward to high school.

Making good on his promise, David visited Kelly more often. He was amazed that he continued to learn something new each time. In fact, his coworkers gave him grief about his sister being the real brains in his family.

On a couple of occasions, David brought Kelly to Trendex to talk with an emerging leaders group or to guide a team of seasoned leaders through what was now called the "Always Growing" approach. People said the simple analogy really helped them visualize what they needed to do to be stronger leaders, whether they had been in the role for one year or 20 years.

One day when he and Amy drove to Kelly's place, David noticed Kelly talking with a group of people. Amy went inside the store to check out what was new, and David walked to where the group was meeting. They were just finishing up when Kelly saw David.

"You're too late; the tour is over," she said as she hugged David.

"Tour?" he asked. "Since when do you give tours?"

"Since I realized I need to share my love of growing in a different way," she replied. "Anything I can do now to help instill a desire within others to grow vegetables or plant a fruit tree in their back yard would seem to be time well spent."

David smiled and said, "It all goes back to your favorite quote, doesn't it?"

"Yes," was Kelly's quick reply. "You are *always* a gardener. Every moment contains the opportunity to help something or, as you now know, *someone* grow in some way. Because of age or other circumstances, I may not be as active as I once was, but I can always do *something*."

Beginning to walk, Kelly said, "Let's revisit something."

Kelly and David walked past the spot where their grandfather's old barn had once stood. A newer one had taken its place. They stopped where the row of overgrown apple trees had once stood. Only one tree remained now.

"Remember all the trees that were in this row?" Kelly asked. "Imagine all the apples they could have produced if they had been given the right environment for growth," she said longingly. "If I had taken the time to cultivate them – if they had been pruned properly – think about the results they *could* have had. But because I lost sight of them for a little while, they were practically useless.

"I've learned that **when you choose to stop growing, you miss the opportunity to produce some incredible results.** In my case, I chose creating this business and nurturing strong relationships with people. You chose growing people at Trendex. Others might choose to inspire students in the classroom or develop a cure for a disease or simply be the best spouse or parent they can be. You just never know what can happen when you make the choice to always grow yourself and those around you."

When you choose to stop growing,
you miss the opportunity to produce
some incredible results.

As they turned to walk back toward the office, David smiled at Kelly. Her tan face and infectious grin still showed the exuberance of the little girl who at an early age found a way to lead herself and others to something better.

David was glad he had discovered how to become a stronger leader, too – even if he did have to give some credit to his big sister.

LIFE TIP

- When you choose to stop growing, you miss the opportunity to produce some incredible results.

It's Time
To Get *Growing!*

Always Growing

You are always a gardener.
What grows — and how it grows — is up to you.

Grow

- Identify what you can and cannot control, and invest your time where you can have the greatest return.
- Letting something grow on its own doesn't always bring the desired result.
- Create the environment that gives a plant the best chance to grow.
- Determine what a plant needs for optimum growth.
- A plant will only grow as fast as its most limiting factor.
- A plant needs the right temperature to encourage it to grow.

What three words describe the environment you create for your team?
Do you communicate the vision and your team's mission in a meaningful way?
Do you anticipate what your team members need to deliver their best work?
Are you in touch with what motivates each individual?

Cultivate

- Cultivation is required to stay focused on what you want to grow.
- Preventing the weeds from growing limits their ability to use resources.
- Continually evaluate your methods to see if they are making the best use of your resources.
- Time spent seeking advice and sharing ideas always helps you improve what you're growing.

Where does your focus need to be right now?
What are three "weeds" competing with your team's highest priorities?
What routines or activities should you engage in more often?
*Who are three people who could help **you** grow?*

Prune

- You sometimes have to say no to things of lesser importance so you can say yes to things of greater importance.
- Pruning is a reallocation of resources to nurture the desired growth.
- Pruning frees up resources that can be used in the areas of greatest importance.
- Pruning is most critical in the early stages of growth because you're forming the structure for the future.
- Prune at the first signs of undesirable outcomes.

Where do you feel like things are growing out of control for you or your team?
Are there tasks expected of your team that are not directly related to the mission?
How can you change your priorities to provide an extra hour for you to use each week to improve your effectiveness as a leader?
What benefits arise if you better manage the expectations of yourself and your team?

Harvest

- Harvest is about much more than the numbers.
- Harvest is when you celebrate ALL of your productive results.
- Reflect on the results of your efforts rather than just on what you're trying to grow.
- You have to be intentional about celebrating your harvest moments as well as focusing on what you're trying to grow.

Do you focus more on what is getting done or what is not getting done?
What are three small accomplishments you should be celebrating with your team?
Where else do you see your team members making small progress?
Who needs you to celebrate a harvest moment with them right now?

When you choose to stop growing,
you miss the opportunity to produce some incredible results.

About The Author

JONES LOFLIN is president of Helping Others Prepare for Excellence Inc., a speaking and training organization that focuses on growing leaders by teaching them to prioritize their responsibilities, efficiently manage their time, quickly embrace change, and find a rewarding balance between work and life. Jones is an internationally-recognized speaker and author, having presented in all 50 states and eight countries.

For over 22 years Jones has focused on creating innovative yet practical solutions for his clients, which range from Fortune 100 companies and trade associations to government agencies and education groups. His past work also includes serving as the "Trainer of Trainers" for the best-selling book, *Who Moved My Cheese?*

Always Growing is Jones' fourth book. His other books include: *Juggling Elephants* – a witty parable offering solutions to the struggle of too much to do; *Getting the Blue Ribbon* – a process to find greater success in times of change; and *Getting to It* – a field guide to accomplishing what's most important in your work and life.

Jones lives in North Carolina with his incredible wife Lisa, and their two perfect daughters, Alex and Sydney.

To learn more about Jones, his books, or resources related to *Always Growing*, visit www.jonesloflin.com or call 800-853-4676.

Twitter:	@jonesloflin
Facebook:	wjonesloflin
LinkedIn:	/in/jonesloflin

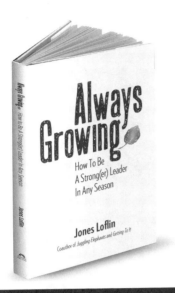

To learn more about products and services for individuals and organizations based on *Always Growing*, visit: www.alwaysgrowingbook.com or call:
1-800-853-4676
336-859-9862 (International)

Bring Jones Loflin to Your Organization

With his innovative yet practical solutions, Jones Loflin is the perfect choice to make your next conference or training event unforgettable. His simple strategies related to leadership, time management, change, and motivation will equip your people to deliver their best work.

To bring Jones Loflin to your organization, visit www.jonesloflin.com or call 336-859-9862.